Keeping it Simple

Keeping it Simple

New recipes from the Caravan Chef

Eva Stovern

 SBS  hardie grant publishing

Contents

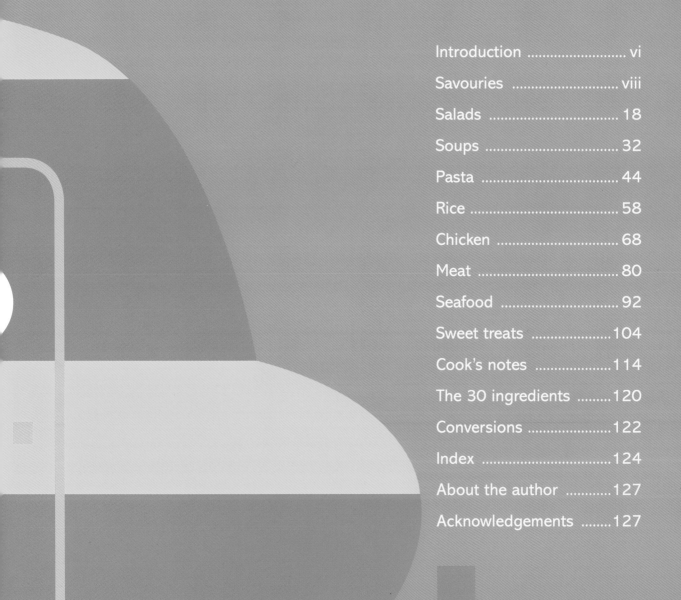

Introduction

Many of you may know me as 'the Caravan Chef', a happy fellow traveller who also loves to cook; however, I'm also a wife, mother and grandmother, living in the suburbs of bustling Sydney, Australia. When I cook at home, my motto is the same as when I'm on the road: keep it simple, use few utensils, and above all, make it tasty and healthy. I also make sure that the 30 ingredients listed in my previous cookbooks are always in my pantry.

When writing this cookbook, I delighted in choosing a new set of ingredients from the vast assortment available. I indulged in a selection of exotic cheeses, such as fresh goat's cheese and haloumi, and I loved browsing the colourful selection of fresh fruit and vegetables.

Lately, the public has been introduced to the benefits of cooking with 'super foods'. I've taken that advice on board and included many of them in my recipes. The section on seafood includes mussels and salmon, which are known to be rich in omega-3.

A big thank you to my followers; you've enriched my life with your generous praise, travel stories and cooking experiences. Some of you have become more like friends: Kenn from Melbourne, thank you for taking the 'Caravan Chef' journey to the max by cooking every single recipe; Carla from Tasmania, for calling my book her 'little cooking bible'; and to the many people who have told me that my cookbooks have motivated them to start cooking for the very first time. Your loyalty has inspired me to continue cooking and creating yummy recipes.

Bon appétit

Eva

Savouries

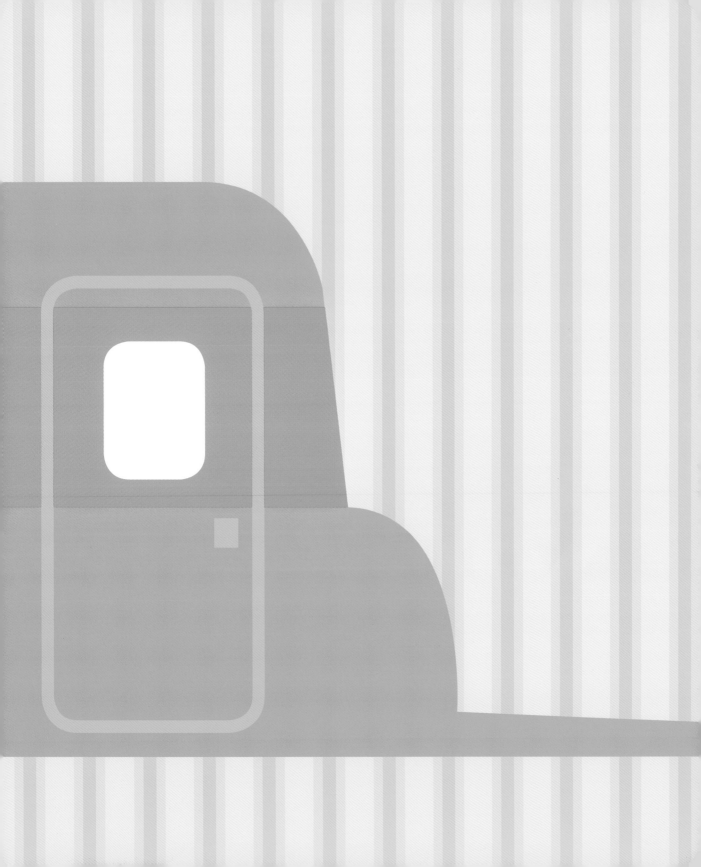

How to make shortcrust pastry

Ingredients

120 g (1 cup) plain (all-purpose) flour, extra for rolling out
65 g butter, cut into small cubes
4 tablespoons cold water
olive oil spray
200 g (1 cup) uncooked rice, for blind baking

Method

1. Sift the flour into a large bowl.

2. Using your fingertips rub the butter into the flour, until the mixture resembles breadcrumbs.

(3) Add the water a little at a time. Mix with a knife using cutting motions, until a dough forms. Discard any leftover water.

(4) Work the dough lightly with your hands and shape into a ball. Wrap the dough in cling wrap and refrigerate for at least 15 minutes, as resting the dough makes rolling out easier. If making the pastry in advance, the wrapped ball of dough can be refrigerated for up to two days, or frozen for up to two months.

(5) To cook the pastry, preheat a fan-forced oven to 180°C (conventional oven 200°C/Gas 4).

(6) Lightly spray the inside of a 25 cm pie dish with olive oil spray.

(7) Using a rolling pin, on a lightly floured surface, roll out the dough, until slightly wider than the diameter of the pie dish. Place the dough evenly over the pie dish and trim.

(8) Cover the dough with baking paper extending past the edges and fill with the uncooked rice. Blind bake for 10 minutes.

(9) Lift out the paper and rice. Bake for an additional 5 minutes, until lightly golden. Remove from the oven.

(10) The pastry shell is ready to make a savoury quiche, sweet pie or leftovers recipe.

How to roast pumpkin

55 MINUTES • MAKES 2 CUPS

Ingredients

750 g butternut pumpkin, skin removed
1 tablespoon extra-virgin olive oil
salt and freshly ground black pepper

Method

1 Preheat a fan-forced oven to 190°C (conventional oven 210°C/Gas 5). Cut the pumpkin into large bite-sized pieces.

2 In a small bowl mix the pumpkin with the oil, ensuring that the pumpkin is well coated.

3 Distribute the pumpkin pieces evenly on a baking tray, without overlapping. Bake, turning occasionally, for 30–40 minutes, until lightly browned and tender.

4 Remove from the oven, then season with the salt and pepper.

5 Serve as a side dish or add to soups, salads and antipasti. The pumpkin can be roasted in advance and refrigerated for up to two days.

How to caramelise onions

Ingredients

65 ml (¼ cup) extra-virgin olive oil
750 g brown onions, evenly sliced
4 tablespoons raw sugar
1 tablespoon balsamic vinegar

Method

1. In a medium saucepan heat the oil over medium heat. Add the onions, stir to coat and bring to a light sizzle. Lower the heat and cook, stirring occasionally, for 15 minutes, until the onions wilt and just start to brown. Scrape any browned bits from the bottom of the pan and mix with the onions.

2. Add the sugar and simmer, stirring occasionally, for 20 minutes, until the onions brown and the liquid reduces.

3 Add the balsamic vinegar and cook until it starts to bubble. Stir, scraping the bottom of the pan to deglaze.

4 Simmer for a further 10 minutes, stirring occasionally.

5 Serve as a side dish or over meat, seafood, pasta, pizza or salad.

Chicken and broccoli quiche

65 MINUTES • SERVES 4

Ingredients

1 quantity shortcrust pastry (*see* p. 2, steps 1–4), at room temperature
olive oil spray
200 g (1 cup) uncooked rice, for blind baking
100 g (1⅔ cup) broccoli, cut into florets
150 g chicken thigh fillets, cut into bite-sized pieces
3 eggs
300 ml cream
salt and freshly ground black pepper

Method

1 Preheat a fan-forced oven to 180°C (conventional oven 200°C/Gas 4). Lightly spray the inside of a 25 cm pie dish with olive oil spray.

2 Using a rolling pin, on a lightly floured surface, roll out the dough, until slightly wider than the diameter of the pie dish. Place the dough evenly over the pie dish and trim.

3 Cover the dough with baking paper extending past the edges and fill with uncooked rice. Blind bake the pastry shell for 10 minutes. Lift out the paper and rice, and bake the shell for a further 5 minutes, until lightly golden. Remove from the oven and set aside.

4 Reduce the oven temperature to 170°C (conventional oven 190°C/Gas 3).

5 Cook the broccoli in boiling water for 4 minutes, then drain.

6 Meanwhile, heat a medium non-stick frying pan and spray lightly with olive oil spray. Add the chicken and sauté over high heat for 2 minutes, until browned all over. Remove from the pan and place onto paper towels. Set aside to cool slightly.

7 In a medium bowl whisk the eggs with the cream and set aside.

8 Distribute the chicken and broccoli evenly over the cooked pastry shell, then season with the salt and pepper.

9 Pour the egg mixture evenly over the top. Bake for 30–35 minutes, until the egg mixture has set and the quiche is lightly browned on top. Set aside to cool.

10 Slice the quiche into wedges and serve with a green salad.

Ham and potato pie

Ingredients

400 g potatoes, peeled and halved
2 eggs, lightly beaten
125 ml (½ cup) cream
olive oil spray
2 quantities shortcrust pastry dough (*see* p. 2, steps 1–4), at room temperature
200 g ham, diced
1 medium white onion, sliced into thin rings
salt and freshly ground black pepper

Method

1. Bring a medium saucepan of water to the boil. Add the potatoes, cover with a lid, lower the heat to medium and cook for 10–12 minutes, until tender.

2. Meanwhile, in a medium bowl whisk the eggs with the cream and set aside.

3. Preheat a fan-forced oven to 190°C (conventional oven 210°C/Gas 5). Lightly spray the inside of a 25 cm pie dish with olive oil spray.

4. Using a rolling pin, on a lightly floured surface, roll out the dough into two pastry sheets. Place one of the sheets evenly over the base of the pie dish and trim.

5. Drain the potatoes. Using tongs to avoid the heat, thinly slice the potato halves.

6. Arrange the potatoes evenly on the bottom of the pie dish. Repeat with a layer of ham and onion, then season with the salt and pepper.

7. Pour the egg mixture evenly over the top, retaining enough to brush the top of the pie pastry. Lift the potatoes with a fork to allow the egg mixture to flow down to the base.

8. Cover the pie with the remaining pastry sheet and trim to fit. With a fork press around the edge of the pie to seal, and pierce six vent holes in the pie top. Brush with the remaining egg mixture and bake for 30–35 minutes, until browned on top.

9. Allow the pie to cool slightly, by then the eggs will have set, making it easier to cut. Slice into wedges and serve with vegetables or a salad.

Caramelised onion and feta omelette

Ingredients

2 teaspoons extra-virgin olive oil
3 eggs, lightly whisked
⅓ quantity caramelised onions (*see* p. 6)
100 g feta, diced
salt and freshly ground black pepper
fresh parsley, coarsely chopped to garnish

Method

1 In a medium non-stick frying pan heat the oil over medium–high heat. Pour in the eggs and cook for 2 minutes, until the base starts to set to form an omelette. Shake the pan occasionally to prevent sticking.

2 Arrange the caramelised onions evenly over half of the omelette. Sprinkle the feta on top of the onions, and season with the salt and pepper.

3 Fold over the remaining half of the omelette. Cook for a further 2 minutes, until the feta has softened and the folded half has set as well.

4 Top with the parsley and serve with a green salad.

Asparagus and feta quiche

Ingredients

olive oil spray
1 quantity shortcrust pastry (*see* p. 2, steps 1–4), at room temperature
200 g (1 cup) uncooked rice, for blind baking
1 bunch asparagus spears, chopped
3 eggs, lightly beaten
300 ml cream
150 g feta, cut into small cubes
salt and freshly ground black pepper

Method

1. Preheat a fan-forced oven to 180°C (conventional oven 200°C/Gas 4). Lightly spray the inside of a 25 cm pie dish with olive oil spray.

2. Using a rolling pin, on a lightly floured surface, roll out the dough, until slightly wider than the diameter of the pie dish. Place the pastry dough evenly over the pie dish and trim.

3. Cover the dough with baking paper, extending past the edges and fill with uncooked rice. Bake the pastry shell for 10 minutes. Lift out the paper and rice, and bake the shell for a further 5 minutes, until lightly golden. Remove from the oven and set aside.

4. Meanwhile, cook the asparagus in rapidly boiling water for 2 minutes, until lightly cooked. Drain and leave to cool slightly.

5. Reduce the oven temperature to 170°C (conventional oven 190°C/Gas 3).

6. In a medium bowl whisk the eggs with the cream and set aside.

7. Distribute the asparagus and feta evenly over the cooked pastry shell, then season with the salt and pepper.

8. Pour the egg mixture evenly over the top. Bake for 30–35 minutes, until the egg mixture has set and the quiche is lightly browned on top.

9. Slice the quiche into wedges when slightly cooled, by then the eggs will have set, making it easier to cut. Serve with a green salad.

Ham and eggs over potatoes

Ingredients

500 g potatoes, peeled and diced
salt (optional)
1 bunch asparagus spears, halved lengthwise
150 g smoked ham, diced
1 teaspoon extra-virgin olive oil
2 garlic cloves, chopped
2 eggs

Method

1. Cook the potatoes in a large saucepan of boiling salted water for 7 minutes. Add the asparagus and cook over medium heat for 5 minutes, until the vegetables are tender.

2. Meanwhile, heat a medium non-stick frying pan and sauté the ham over medium–high heat for 2–3 minutes, until crisp and lightly browned. Remove from the pan and set aside.

3. Add the oil and garlic to the frying pan and sauté over low heat for 1 minute, until just sizzling and fragrant. Remove from the pan and set aside

4. Drain the potatoes and asparagus. Separate the asparagus and set aside.

5. Return the potatoes to the saucepan, add the garlic, and mash them together.

6. Return the frying pan to medium heat. Add the eggs and cook sunny-side up for 2–3 minutes, until lightly cooked.

7. To serve, make a bed of mash and top with the ham, asparagus and eggs.

Haloumi salad

Ingredients

180 g haloumi, sliced into ½ cm pieces
olive oil spray
15 g (½ cup) basil leaves
200 g grape tomato medley, halved
125 g can chickpeas, drained
2 teaspoons extra-virgin olive oil
2 teaspoons lime juice, freshly squeezed
½ teaspoon raw sugar
salt and freshly ground black pepper

Method

1. Dry the haloumi on paper towels to remove excess moisture.

2. Heat a medium non-stick frying pan and lightly spray with olive oil spray. Add the haloumi, without overlapping, and cook over medium heat for 1–2 minutes on each side, until golden.

3. Meanwhile, in a medium bowl combine the basil, tomatoes and chickpeas, and set aside.

4. In a separate small bowl combine the oil, lime juice and sugar to make a dressing. Pour the dressing over the salad, then season with the salt and pepper.

5. Serve the salad on individual plates and top with the haloumi.

Roast pumpkin and goat's cheese salad

5 MINUTES • SERVES 2

Ingredients

½ quantity roast pumpkin (*see* p. 4)
150 g goat's cheese, cut into cubes
60 g (1⅓ cups) baby rocket
150 g grape tomatoes, halved
½ small red onion, sliced into rings
2 tablespoons pine nuts
65 ml (¼ cup) balsamic dressing
salt and freshly ground black pepper

Method

1. In a medium bowl lightly toss the roast pumpkin, cheese, rocket, tomatoes and onion.

2. Sprinkle with the pine nuts and drizzle with the dressing.

3. Season the salad with the salt and pepper.
   Serve as a salad or as a side dish.

Simple tasty coleslaw

Ingredients

¼ small cabbage, finely shredded
2 small carrots, coarsely grated
2 small green apples, peeled and coarsely grated
1 medium white onion, finely chopped
2 tablespoons olive oil vinaigrette
2 teaspoons raw sugar
salt and freshly ground black pepper

Method

1. In a medium bowl place the cabbage, carrots, apples, onion, vinaigrette, sugar, and lightly stir until combined.

2. Season the salad with the salt and pepper. Serve as an appetiser or as a side dish.

Warm chicken with quick noodle salad

Ingredients

1 x 85 g packet instant chicken noodles
2 teaspoons cornflour
4 teaspoons soy sauce
300 g chicken loin fillets
1 teaspoon extra-virgin olive oil
2 teaspoons sweet chilli sauce
4 medium iceberg lettuce leaves, shredded
salt and freshly ground black pepper

Method

1. Break the noodles into small pieces. Cook with the seasoning, as per the packet instructions, and then drain.

2. Spread the cooked noodles evenly on a flat surface to dry.

3. Meanwhile, in a medium bowl combine the cornflour with half of the soy sauce. Add the chicken and mix until coated.

4. Heat the oil in a medium non-stick frying pan. Add the chicken and cook over medium heat for 2–3 minutes on each side, until browned and cooked through. Remove from the pan and slice into thin strips.

5. In a large bowl mix the remaining soy sauce with the sweet chilli sauce. Add the lettuce, chicken and noodles, and mix until coated with the sauce.

6. Season the salad with the salt and pepper, and serve.

Greek salad

Ingredients

1 medium Lebanese cucumber, quartered lengthwise and thickly sliced
1 medium tomato, diced
1 small red onion, sliced into rings
150 g feta, cut into cubes
80 g (½ cup) pitted kalamata olives, drained
2 tablespoons olive oil vinaigrette
salt and freshly ground black pepper
3 medium iceberg lettuce leaves, shredded (optional)

Method

1. In a medium bowl place the cucumber, tomato, onion, feta, olives and vinaigrette. Stir lightly until combined.

2. Season the salad with the salt and pepper.

3. Serve on top of the shredded lettuce, if using, for extra colour.

Kipfler potato salad

Ingredients

2 eggs
450 g kipfler potatoes
3 small pickled dill cucumbers, sliced
2 medium tomatoes, diced
1 small white onion, sliced into rings
3 tablespoons olive oil vinaigrette
salt and freshly ground black pepper

Method

1 Submerge the eggs in a saucepan of cold water. Bring to the boil, lower the heat to medium and cook for 8 minutes. Rinse under cold water. Peel and cut into wedges.

2 Meanwhile, cook the potatoes in boiling water for 10–12 minutes, until tender, then drain and set aside to cool slightly. Slice the potatoes into rounds.

3 In a medium bowl place the potatoes, dill cucumbers, tomatoes and onions. Lightly mix to combine.

4 Portion onto serving plates and arrange the eggs on top.

5 Pour over the vinaigrette and season with the salt and pepper.

6 Serve as a salad or as a side dish.

Smoked salmon salad

10 MINUTES • SERVES 2

Ingredients

3 medium iceberg lettuce leaves, shredded
45 g (1 cup) baby rocket
150 g grape tomatoes, halved
½ small red onion, thinly sliced
2 small pickled dill cucumbers, sliced
100 g smoked salmon slices
2 tablespoons baby capers, drained
2 tablespoons extra-virgin olive oil
2 tablespoons lime juice, freshly squeezed
salt and freshly ground black pepper

Method

1. In a medium bowl gently mix the lettuce with the rocket.

2. Make a bed of the mixed leaves on serving plates. Top with the tomatoes, onion and dill cucumbers.

3. Arrange the salmon slices on top, dot with capers and drizzle with the olive oil and lime juice.

4. Season with the salt and pepper, and serve.

Soups

Light chicken soup

Ingredients

1 chicken breast bone
2 chicken drumsticks, skinless
1 stick celery, sliced into ½ cm pieces
1 medium carrot, diced
½ small brown onion, chopped
2 bay leaves
1 litre (4 cups) chicken stock
salt and freshly ground black pepper
fresh parsley, coarsley chopped to garnish

Method

1 In a large saucepan place the chicken bone, drumsticks, celery, carrot, onion, bay leaves and stock. Cover with a lid and bring to the boil.

2 Lower the heat and simmer for 30 minutes, until the chicken cooks through and starts to separate from the bone. Remove the pot from the stove and season with the salt and pepper.

3 Remove the chicken pieces from the broth and set aside for 5 minutes to cool.

4 Strip any chicken meat away from the bone. Discard the bones and return the meat to the broth. Sprinkle with the parsley and serve.

Beetroot soup

Ingredients

425 g can diced beetroot, drained reserving the juice
1 medium cucumber, peeled and diced
500 ml (2 cups) chicken stock
salt and freshly ground black pepper
60 ml (¼ cup) cream
chives, chopped to garnish (optional)

Method

1. Place the beetroot in a medium saucepan, together with 125 ml (½ cup) of the reserved juice. Add the cucumber and chicken stock. Bring to the boil.

2. Lower the heat and simmer for 10 minutes, stirring occasionally, until the cucumber colours red. Remove from heat and set aside for 30 minutes, until cool.

3. Place the vegetables and broth into an electric blender, in batches if necessary, and puree.

4. Season the soup with the salt and pepper, and stir in the cream.

5. Serve the soup hot or cold, topped with the chives, if using.

Roast pumpkin and tomato soup

40 MINUTES PLUS COOLING TIME • SERVES 2

Ingredients

400 g butternut pumpkin, cut into bite-sized pieces
1 tablespoon extra-virgin olive oil
3 small ripe tomatoes, cut into wedges
1 small red onion, cut into wedges
2 garlic cloves, chopped
500 ml (2 cups) vegetable or chicken stock
salt and freshly ground black pepper
125 ml (½ cup) cream

Method

1. Preheat a fan-forced oven to 200°C (conventional oven 220°C/Gas 6).

2. In a medium bowl mix the pumpkin with 2 teaspoons of the oil. Transfer to a baking dish and spread out evenly. Bake for 10 minutes.

3. Meanwhile, place the tomatoes, onion, garlic and remaining oil in the bowl and stir to combine.

4. Remove the baking dish from the oven and add the tomato mixture to the pumpkin, without overlapping.

5. Continue baking, turning occasionally, for 20 minutes, until the vegetables are tender and the pumpkin has browned.

6. Remove the vegetables from the oven and set aside for 20 minutes, until cooled. Peel off and discard any loose skins from the tomatoes.

7. Puree the vegetables in an electric blender with the stock, in batches if necessary, and season with the salt and pepper. Stir in the cream and serve.

Creamy vegetable soup

Ingredients

2 teaspoons extra-virgin olive oil
1 small brown onion, chopped
1 garlic clove, chopped
1 small red sweet potato, diced
1 small carrot, diced
1 stick celery, sliced into ½ cm pieces
1 small broccoli, chopped
2 tablespoons peas, fresh, frozen or freeze-dried
1 litre (4 cups) vegetable or chicken stock
85 g (½ cup) risoni pasta
salt and freshly ground black pepper
60 ml (¼ cup) cream

Method

1. Heat the oil in a medium saucepan over low heat and sauté the onion for 2 minutes, until it softens.

2. Add the garlic, sauté for 1 minute, until the garlic is fragrant but not brown.

3. Add the sweet potato, carrot, celery, broccoli, peas and stock. Bring to the boil. Cover with a lid, lower the heat and simmer for 7 minutes, stirring occasionally.

4. Add the risoni, season with the salt and pepper, and stir. Return to the boil. Lower the heat and simmer, covered, for 7 minutes, until the pasta is cooked. Stir in the cream and serve.

Mixed berries soup

Ingredients

50 g (½ cup) small noodles
450 g can mixed berries, drained reserving the juice
1 punnet strawberries, sliced
125 ml (½ cup) cream
1 teaspoon sugar (optional)

Method

1 Cook the noodles as per the packet instructions. Drain.

2 Meanwhile, place the juice from the can of berries and the fresh strawberries in a medium saucepan. Bring to the boil. Lower the heat and simmer for 3 minutes, stirring occasionally, until the strawberries are tender.

3 Remove from heat and stir in the drained mixed berries. Set aside for 30 minutes, until cool.

4 Add the cream and noodles, and mix to combine. Stir in the sugar, if using.

5 Serve the soup as an entree, warm or cold.

How to cook pasta

Ingredients

2 litres (8 cups) water
1 tablespoon salt
200 g pasta
250 ml (1 cup) cold water

Method

1 In a large saucepan bring the water to a rapid boil. Add the salt. Do NOT add oil to the water.

2 Add the pasta. Do not break long pasta. Instead, stand the long strands on the side of the saucepan, and gently push them down as they soften, until they bend in the middle and become completely immersed.

3 Add the cold water to help stop the pasta from sticking, then return to the boil.

4 Stir the pasta occasionally, to separate. Cook to al dente: cooked but slightly firm. On average that should take about 8–10 minutes for dried pasta, and 2–3 minutes for fresh pasta. However, time may vary according to the type of pasta and for best results follow the instructions on the packet.

5 Always have the sauce ready by the time the pasta is cooked. Sauce is most flavoursome when served over freshly cooked pasta.

6 When draining pasta, save a cup of the cooking water to add to the pasta sauce. Use your judgement as to the amount, on average add 60 ml (¼ cup). Or transfer the pasta to the plates or the sauce using tongs, as they capture some of the cooking liquid in the process. The water will enhance the flavour of the sauce. Do NOT rinse cooked pasta.

7 Freshly grated parmesan is the best cheese to use with pasta, however hard cheddar is also suitable. It may be added to the pasta before the sauce. Freshly ground black pepper is also great over the sauce.

Roast vegetable penne

Ingredients

1 small carrot, sliced
1 small red capsicum, coarsely chopped
1 tablespoon extra-virgin olive oil
1 small zucchini (courgette), sliced into thick rounds
1 medium tomato, cut into wedges
1 small red onion, cut into wedges
200 g penne
20 g (½ cup) baby rocket
40 g (½ cup) parmesan, freshly grated
salt and freshly ground black pepper

Method

1 Preheat a fan-forced oven to 200°C (conventional oven 220°C/Gas 6).

2 In a medium bowl mix the carrot, capsicum and half the oil. Transfer to a baking dish without overlapping the vegetables. Bake for 10 minutes.

3 Meanwhile, place the zucchini (courgette), tomato, onion and remaining oil into the mixing bowl. Stir gently until coated.

4 Remove the baking dish from the oven. Add the zucchini (courgette) mixture, making sure no vegetables overlap. Continue baking for 20 minutes, turning occasionally, until the vegetables are tender.

5 Meanwhile, cook the pasta to al dente (see p. 46), or as per the packet instructions. Drain the pasta, reserving 60 ml (¼ cup) of the liquid.

6 Remove the baking dish from the oven. Lift and discard any loose skins from the tomatoes.

7 Add the pasta liquid and the rocket to the baking dish and mix through. Sprinkle with the parmesan, season with the salt and pepper, and serve.

Fettuccine with mushrooms and bacon

Ingredients

200 g fettuccine
1 tablespoon extra-virgin olive oil
1 small white onion, diced
100 g lean bacon, diced
200 g button mushrooms, sliced
1 tablespoon fresh parsley, coarsely chopped
150 ml cream
60 g (¾ cup) parmesan cheese, freshly grated
salt and freshly ground black pepper

Method

1. Cook the pasta to al dente (*see* p. 46), or as per the packet instructions.

2. Meanwhile, heat the oil in a deep non-stick frying pan and sauté the onion over medium heat for 1 minute, until fragrant. Add the bacon and sauté for 1 minute, until the onion is soft.

3. Add the mushrooms and parsley and sauté for 2 minutes, until the mushrooms cook and lightly brown. Add the cream and parmesan, cook for 1 minute, stirring, until the cheese melts.

4. Using tongs, transfer the pasta, as well as some of the water, to the frying pan and combine with the sauce. Season with the salt and pepper, and serve.

Spaghetti with tomatoes and rocket

15 MINUTES • SERVES 2

Ingredients

200 g spaghetti
2 tablespoons extra-virgin olive oil
1 garlic clove, chopped
250 g cherry tomato medley, halved
45 g (1 cup) baby rocket
salt and freshly ground black pepper
40 g (½ cup) parmesan, freshly grated (optional)

Method

1. Cook the pasta to al dente (*see* p. 46), or as per the packet instructions.

2. Meanwhile, heat the oil in a deep non-stick frying pan. Add the garlic and sauté over low heat for 30 seconds, until the garlic is fragrant but not brown. Stir in the tomatoes and remove the pan from the heat.

3. Using tongs, transfer the pasta, as well as some of the cooking water, to the frying pan. Add the rocket, season with the salt and pepper, and mix until combined. Top with the parmesan, if using, and serve.

Linguini with prawns

Ingredients

200 g linguini
4 tablespoons extra-virgin olive oil
3 garlic cloves, chopped
1 tablespoon fresh parsley, finely chopped
½ teaspoon chilli paste, or to taste
1 teaspoon raw sugar
10 large green prawns, peeled and de-veined
salt and freshly ground black pepper

Method

1. Cook the pasta to al dente (*see* p. 46), or as per the packet instructions.

2. Meanwhile, heat the oil in a deep non-stick frying pan over medium heat. Add the garlic, parsley, chilli paste and sugar. Cook, stirring, for 1 minute, until the garlic is fragrant but not brown.

3. Add the prawns. Lower the heat and cook over low–medium heat for 1 minute on each side, until the prawns change colour.

4. Using tongs, transfer the pasta to the frying pan. Mix until combined with the prawns. Season with the salt and pepper, and serve.

Fettuccine with avocados

12 MINUTES • SERVES 2

Ingredients

200 g fettuccine
1½ tablespoons extra-virgin olive oil
1 garlic clove, chopped
2 medium avocados, diced
salt and freshly ground black pepper
40 g (½ cup) parmesan, grated (optional)

Method

1. Cook the pasta to al dente (*see* p. 46), or as per the packet instructions.

2. Meanwhile, heat the oil and garlic in a deep non-stick frying pan and sauté over low–medium heat for 1 minute, until the garlic is fragrant but not brown.

3. Add the avocados and sauté for 2–3 minutes, to warm through and mix with the oil, then season with the salt and pepper.

4. Using tongs, transfer the pasta, as well as some of the liquid, to the frying pan. Mix until combined. Top with the parmesan, if using, and serve.

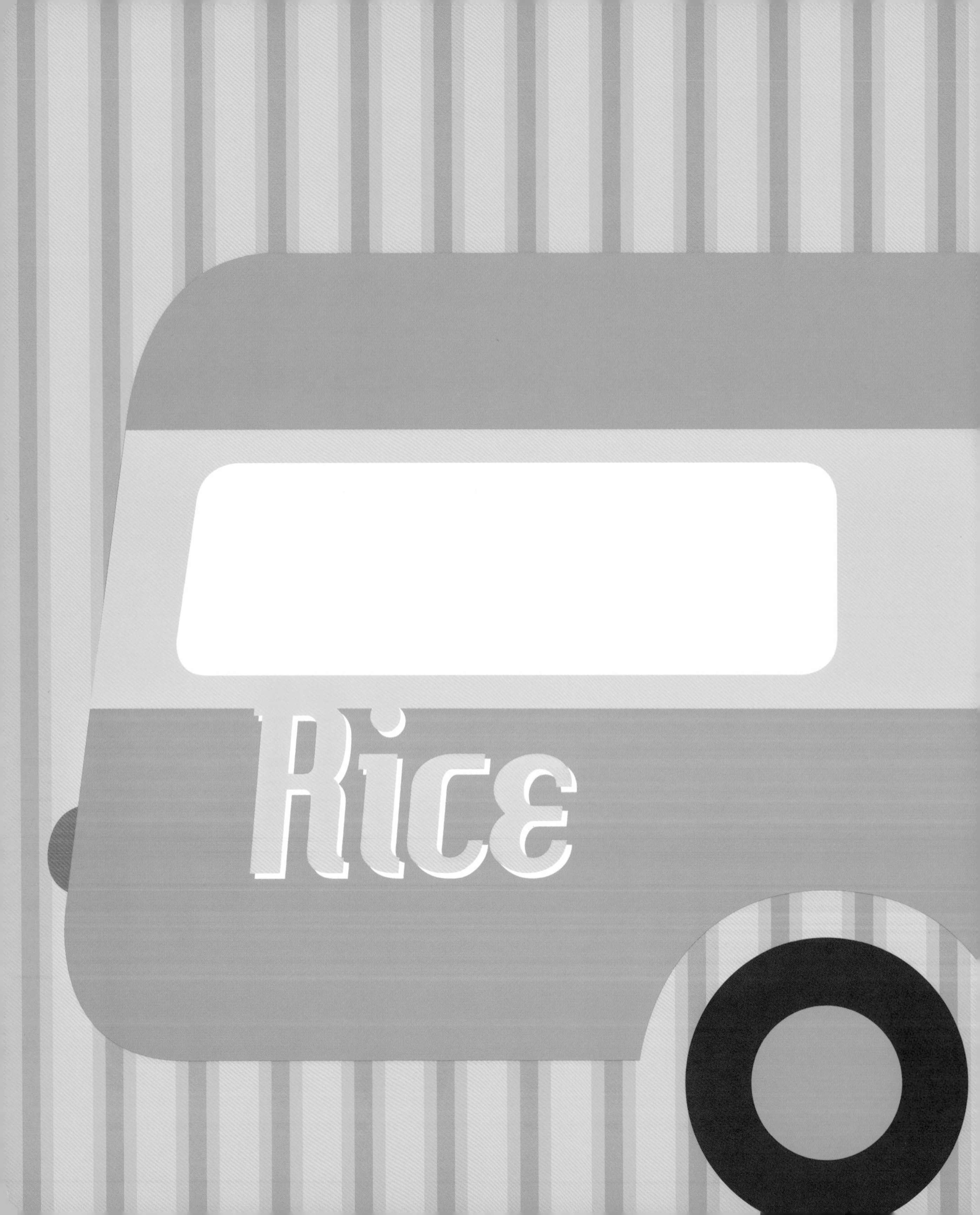
Rice

How to cook rice

Long-grain and basmati rice are popular when cooking pilafs and dishes that require the rice to separate, such as fried rice. Whether boiling or steaming (also known as the absorption method), these rice grains don't need rinsing before cooking, and retain a lovely texture.

For some dishes, such as curries, plain boiled rice is suitable. Cook the rice in plenty of boiling water (salted if desired) for 10–15 minutes, until tender, then drain. For risottos, arborio rice is best. Its grains are creamy and chewy after cooking, due to the high starch content.

Basic steamed rice

20 MINUTES • MAKES 3 CUPS

Ingredients

1 teaspoon extra-virgin olive oil
200 g (1 cup) long-grain rice
500 ml (2 cups) chicken stock
pinch of salt (optional)

Method

1. Heat the oil in a medium saucepan. Add the rice and sauté over medium heat for 1 minute, until the rice is coated in the oil.

2. Stir in the stock, being mindful of hot steam. Cover with a lid and bring to the boil.

3. Lower the heat and simmer, without lifting the lid, for 15 minutes, until the liquid is absorbed and the rice is tender.

4. Fluff the rice with a fork and season with the salt, if using, before serving. The rice can be served on its own or as a side dish.

Mushroom risotto

Ingredients

500 ml (2 cups) chicken stock
125 ml (½ cup) white wine
2 teaspoons extra-virgin olive oil
25 g butter
1 small brown onion, chopped
1 garlic clove, chopped
220 g (1 cup) arborio rice
olive oil spray
200 g button mushrooms, sliced
20 g (¼ cup) parmesan, freshly grated
freshly ground black pepper

Method

1. Mix the stock with the wine and set aside.

2. Heat the oil and half of the butter in a medium saucepan. Add the onion and garlic, and sauté over low heat for 3 minutes, until soft and fragrant.

3. Add the rice and sauté for 1 minute, until the rice is coated in the oil.

4. Add 125 ml (½ cup) of the stock mixture and cook for 2–3 minutes, stirring frequently, until the liquid is absorbed. Repeat the process with another 125 ml (½ cup) of the stock mixture.

5. Meanwhile, heat a medium non-stick frying pan and spray lightly with olive oil spray. Add the mushrooms without overlapping (cook in batches if necessary) and sauté over high heat for 1–2 minutes, until browned on both sides.

6. Transfer the mushrooms to the rice and stir to combine.

7. Add 125 ml (½ cup) of stock mixture to the rice and cook for 2–3 minutes, stirring frequently, until the liquid is absorbed. Repeat the process until all the stock mixture is absorbed and the rice is tender. Stir in the remaining butter and the parmesan. Season with the pepper and serve.

Asparagus risotto

Ingredients

500 ml (2 cups) chicken stock
125 ml (½ cup) white wine
2 teaspoons extra-virgin olive oil
25 g butter
1 small brown onion, chopped
1 garlic clove, chopped
220 g (1 cup) arborio rice
1 bunch asparagus, cut into 1 cm pieces
20 g (¼ cup) parmesan, freshly grated
½ lemon zest, finely grated (optional)
salt and freshly ground black pepper

Method

1. Mix the stock with the wine and set aside.

2. Heat the oil and half of the butter in a medium saucepan. Add the onion and garlic, and sauté over low heat for 3 minutes, until soft and fragrant.

3. Add the rice and sauté for 1 minute, until the rice is coated in the oil.

4. Add 125 ml (½ cup) of the stock mixture and cook for 2–3 minutes, stirring frequently, until the liquid is absorbed. Repeat the process with another 125 ml (½ cup) of the stock mixture.

5. Stir in the asparagus.

6. Add another 125 ml (½ cup) of the stock mixture and cook for 2–3 minutes, stirring frequently, until the liquid is absorbed. Repeat the process until all the stock mixture is absorbed and the asparagus is tender.

7. Stir in the remaining butter, parmesan and lemon, if using. Season with the salt and pepper, and serve.

Chicken and broccoli pilaf

Ingredients

2 teaspoons extra-virgin olive oil
1 small brown onion, diced
100 g (½ cup) basmati rice
375 ml (1½ cups) chicken stock
olive oil spray
250 g chicken thigh fillets, cut into bite-sized pieces
250 g broccoli, cut into florets with stems diced
2 teaspoons soy sauce
salt and freshly ground black pepper

Method

1. Heat the oil in a medium non-stick frying pan. Add the onion and sauté over low heat for 2 minutes, until tender and fragrant.

2. Add the rice and 250 ml (1 cup) of the stock. Cover with a lid and bring to the boil. Lower the heat and simmer, uninterrupted, for 10 minutes.

3. Meanwhile, heat a shallow non-stick frying pan and spray with olive oil spray. Add the chicken and sauté over high heat for 3 minutes, until golden on all sides. Remove from the pan and set aside on paper towel.

4. Add the cooked chicken, broccoli and remaining stock to the rice, and stir to combine. Cover with a lid and bring to the boil. Lower the heat and simmer for 5 minutes, stirring occasionally, until the chicken, rice and broccoli are tender.

5. In the last 2 minutes of cooking, stir in the soy. Season with the salt and pepper, and serve.

Chicken paprika with macaroni

50 MINUTES • SERVES 2

Ingredients

500 g mixed chicken pieces
1 tablespoon plain (all-purpose) flour
1½ tablespoons extra-virgin olive oil
½ small brown onion, chopped
2 teaspoons paprika
pinch of salt
1 medium red capsicum, diced
1 medium tomato, cut into wedges
250 ml (1 cup) chicken stock
100 g macaroni
2 tablespoons sour cream (optional)

Method

1 Coat the chicken pieces with flour.

2 Heat the oil in a deep non-stick frying pan. Add the onion and sauté over low heat for 1–2 minutes, until lightly golden but not browned.

3 Add the paprika and sauté for 1 minute, until fragrant.

4 Add the chicken and season with the salt. Cook over medium heat for 1–2 minutes, turning occasionally, until the chicken browns on all sides.

5 Add the capsicum, tomato and stock. Cover with a lid. Lower the heat and simmer for 35 minutes, turning the chicken and stirring occasionally.

6 Meanwhile cook the pasta (*see* p. 46), drain and set aside.

7 Remove the chicken from the heat. Stir in the sour cream, if using, for a creamier consistency. Serve over the cooked macaroni. Instead of macaroni the chicken can be served over 150 g (¾ cup) steamed rice (*see* p. 60).

Garlic chicken

Ingredients

350 g chicken breast fillet, sliced into 1 cm thick pieces
1½ tablespoons extra-virgin olive oil
1 tablespoon butter
3 garlic cloves, chopped
1 tablespoon parsley, coarsely chopped
freshly squeezed juice of ½ lemon
salt and freshly ground black pepper
2 slices of lemon

Method

1) Brush the chicken on both sides with ½ tablespoon of the oil.

2) Heat a medium non-stick frying pan. Place the chicken in the pan, without overlapping. Cook over medium–high heat for 2–3 minutes on each side, until lightly browned and cooked through. Remove from the pan and keep warm.

3) Place the remaining oil, butter and garlic in the pan. Lower the heat and cook over low heat for 30 seconds, stirring, until the garlic softens and becomes fragrant without browning.

4) Remove the pan from the heat. Stir in the parsley and lemon juice.

5) Place the chicken on serving plates and season with the salt and pepper. Pour the sauce over the chicken and garnish with sliced lemon. Serve with salad or steamed vegetables on the side.

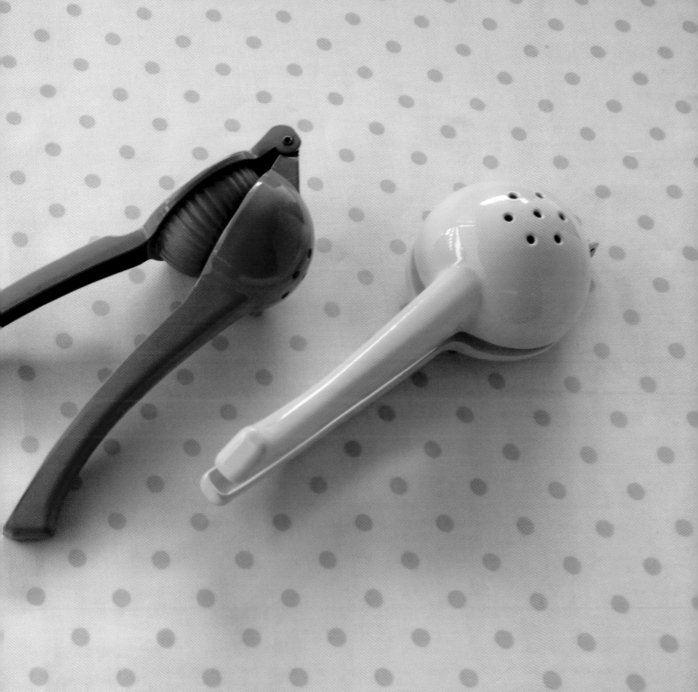

Creamy chicken with potatoes

Ingredients

4 small potatoes, halved
1 tablespoon extra-virgin olive oil
1 small white onion, chopped
1 garlic clove, finely chopped
300 g chicken breast fillets, sliced into thin strips
125 ml (½ cup) cream
100 g (1¼ cups) parmesan, freshly grated
2 teaspoons sweet chilli sauce
1 teaspoon chicken stock powder

Method

1. Cook the potatoes in boiling water for 10–15 minutes, until tender, then drain.

2. Meanwhile, heat the oil in a medium non-stick frying pan. Add the onion and garlic and sauté over low heat for 2 minutes, until soft and lightly browned.

3. Add the chicken to the pan. Increase the heat to high and sauté for 2 minutes, until the chicken lightly browns.

4. Stir in the cream, parmesan, sweet chilli sauce and stock powder. Lower the heat and simmer for 3 minutes, until the parmesan melts and the chicken cooks through.

5. Slice the cooked potatoes and arrange evenly on serving plates. Top with the chicken and the sauce. Season with the salt and pepper, and serve on its own or with a salad.

Apricot chicken with rice
for thermal cooking pots

20 MINUTES PLUS 3 HOURS REST TIME • SERVES 2

Ingredients

100 g (½ cup) long-grain rice
250 ml (1 cup) hot water
3 chicken thigh fillets
2 tablespoons plain (all-purpose) flour
1 tablespoon extra-virgin olive oil
35 g packet French onion soup
425 g can apricot halves in juice
salt and freshly ground black pepper

Method

1. Place the rice and water in the smaller, shallow thermal cooking pot and set aside.

2. Meanwhile, coat the chicken fillets with the flour.

3. Place the oil in the larger, deep thermal cooking pot and heat to a medium temperature. Add the chicken and cook for 1–1½ minutes on each side, until lightly browned all over.

4. Sprinkle the contents of the soup packet over the chicken and pour the tinned apricots, with their juice, over the top. Stir until combined.

5. Fit the small pot with the rice over the large pot with the chicken and cover with a lid.

6. Bring to the boil, lower the heat to medium–low and cook for 10 minutes.

7. Remove from the stove and place inside the thermal host pot. Lock and leave to rest for 3 hours.

8. To serve, make a bed of rice. Place the chicken pieces on the rice and pour the sauce over the top, then season with the salt and pepper.

To see this recipe visit
'Caravan Chef' on YouTube

Chicken and vegetable grill

25 MINUTES • SERVES 2

Ingredients

300 g chicken loin fillets
2 tablespoons extra-virgin olive oil
1 small red capsicum, sliced
1 small carrot, cut lengthwise into thin slices
1 small zucchini, cut lengthwise into thin slices
150 g pumpkin, cut into thin slices
2 tablespoons balsamic salad dressing
salt and freshly ground black pepper

Method

1. Preheat the grill to medium–high.

2. Place the chicken and half of the oil in a medium bowl. Stir until the chicken is coated in the oil and set aside.

3. In another medium bowl place the capsicum, carrot, zucchini and pumpkin with the remaining oil. Mix until combined. Place the vegetables on the grill and cook for 5–6 minutes, turning occasionally, until lightly browned on all sides and slightly undercooked. Move to one side of the grill.

4. Place the chicken, without overlapping, on the other side of the grill and cook for 3 minutes on each side, until lightly browned and cooked through.

5. Meanwhile, continue to turn the vegetables for even cooking.

6. On serving plates make a bed of the grilled vegetables. Place the chicken on top and drizzle with the dressing. Season with the salt and pepper, and serve.

 To see this recipe visit 'Caravan Chef' on YouTube

Chicken with potatoes and asparagus

40 MINUTES • SERVES 2

Ingredients

450 g potatoes, sliced into ½ cm thick pieces
2½ tablespoons extra-virgin olive oil
1 bunch asparagus spears, trimmed and cut into short stems
4 small chicken thigh fillets
4 tablespoons plain (all-purpose) flour
1 garlic clove, finely chopped
125 ml (½ cup) chicken stock
salt and freshly ground black pepper

Method

1. Preheat a fan-forced oven to 190˚C (conventional oven 210˚C/Gas 5).

2. In a medium bowl mix the potatoes with ½ tablespoon of the oil.

3. Spread the potatoes evenly in a baking tray. Bake for 30 minutes, turning and basting, until lightly browned and cooked through.

4. Meanwhile, cook the asparagus in boiling water for 3 minutes, until just tender. Drain and set aside.

5. Coat the chicken with the flour.

6. Heat the remaining oil in a medium non-stick frying pan. Add the chicken and cook over medium heat for 4–5 minutes on each side, until the chicken browns. Stir in the garlic during the last minute of cooking.

7. Add the chicken stock and asparagus to the frying pan and continue cooking over medium heat for 2 minutes, until the chicken is cooked through.

8. On serving plates make a bed of potatoes. Place the chicken on top, add the asparagus and drizzle the sauce from the frying pan over the top. Season with the salt and pepper, and serve.

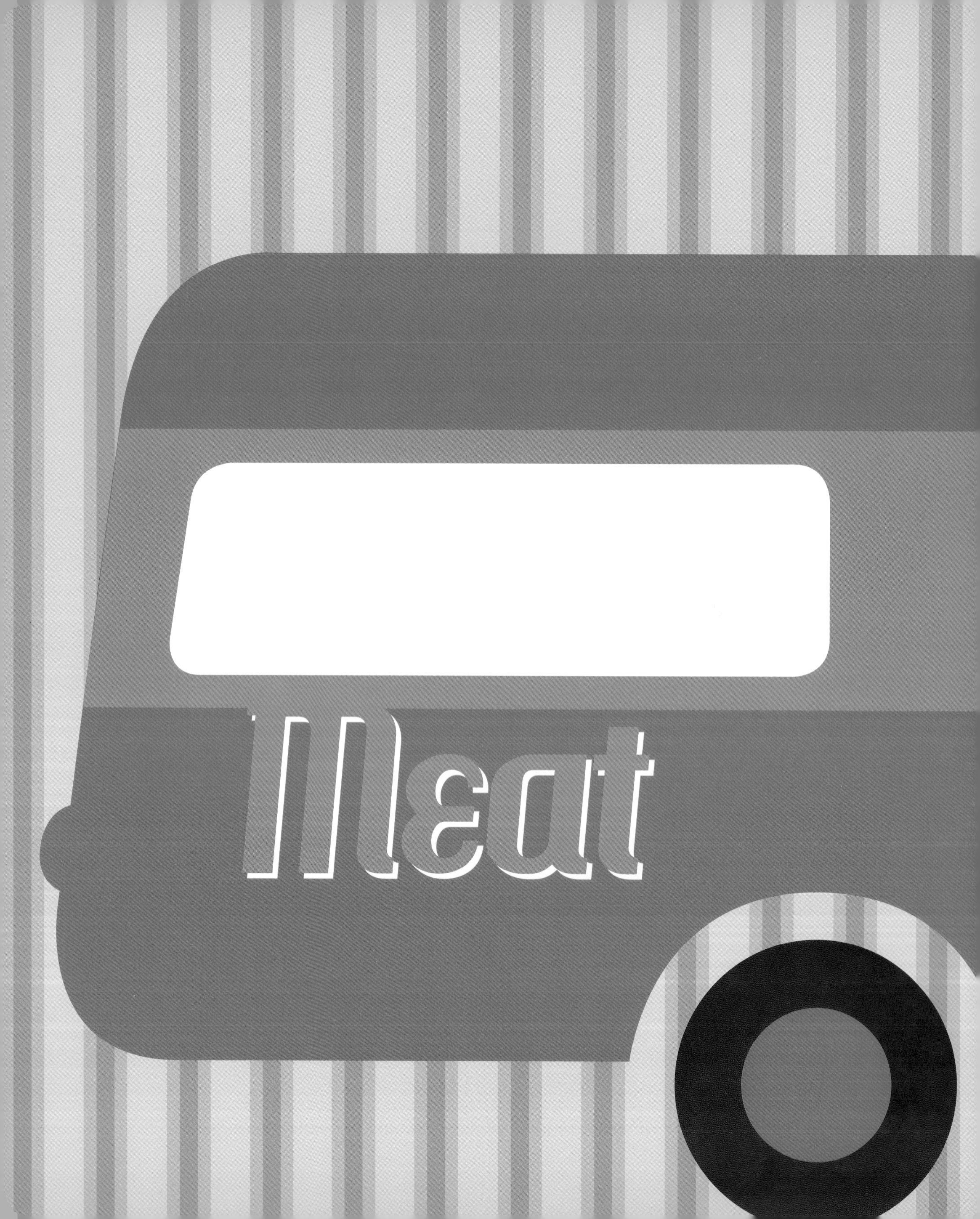
Meat

How to cook a great steak

Ingredients

2 x 175 g Scotch or eye fillet steaks, of even thickness, at least 2 cm
2 teaspoons extra-virgin olive oil
pinch of sea salt
freshly ground black pepper

Method

1 Remove the meat from the fridge 10 minutes prior to cooking. It will help to cook more evenly.

2 Lightly pat the meat dry with paper towel, this will remove excess moisture and help prevent it from stewing.

3 Brush both sides of the steak lightly with the oil. It will help brown the meat, not burn the oil on the surface. Season both sides with salt and pepper just prior to cooking because over time salt draws moisture from the meat.

4 Heat a medium heavy-based frying pan or skillet to high. The meat should sizzle on contact with the surface. (Do not oil the pan.)

5 Take care not to crowd the pan or skillet, as the reduced heat will cause the meat to release juices and stew. (The longer the meat is cooked on a dry heat, the more liquid it loses and the tougher it becomes. In stews and casseroles where the meat is surrounded by liquid, it absorbs the liquid and becomes more tender with longer cooking.)

6 Cook the meat on one side for 1–2 minutes for rare, 2–3 minutes for medium–rare, 4–5 minutes for medium, or 5–6 minutes for well done. Turn once only (with tongs not a fork, to prevent the juices from escaping), and cook the other side for the same amount of time.

7 Before serving, rest the steak for 3–5 minutes. Place it on a clean plate and cover loosely with foil. It will help bring out the flavour. To avoid contamination, do not use the same cookware and utensils to handle uncooked and cooked meat.

Beef curry

65 MINUTES • SERVES 2

Ingredients

500 g beef round steak, cut into large cubes
2 teaspoons plain (all-purpose) flour
1 tablespoon extra-virgin olive oil
1 small brown onion, chopped
1 garlic clove, finely chopped
1 tablespoon curry powder
400 g can diced tomatoes
1 teaspoon raw sugar
250 ml (1 cup) beef stock
salt and freshly ground black pepper
95 g (½ cup) long-grain rice, boiled (*see* p. 60)
3 tablespoons naturally sweet Greek yoghurt, extra to serve
1 banana, sliced (optional)
1 small cucumber, sliced (optional)

Method

1 In a medium bowl coat the meat with the flour.

2 Heat half of the oil in a medium saucepan. Add the meat and sauté over high heat for 3–4 minutes, until browned on all sides. Remove from the pan and set aside.

3 Place the remaining oil, onion and garlic in the pan and sauté over low heat for 1 minute, until fragrant. Add the curry powder and sauté for 1 minute, until fragrant.

4 Return the meat and any juice to the pan and cook over low heat for 1 minute, stirring. Stir in the diced tomatoes and their juice, sugar and stock, and season with the salt and pepper. Bring to the boil. Lower the heat and simmer, stirring occasionally, for 45 minutes, until the meat is tender.

5 Stir in the yoghurt and serve the curry over the rice. Top with the extra yoghurt, banana and cucumber, if using.

Chinese-style grilled lamb

Ingredients

2 teaspoons raw sugar
salt and freshly ground black pepper
2½ teaspoons rice vinegar
3 teaspoons soy sauce
1 garlic clove, finely chopped
300 g lamb backstrap fillet, cut against the grain of the meat into 2 cm steaks
2 teaspoons honey
3 teaspoons sesame oil
4 small lettuce leaves, shredded
1 small zucchini (courgette), coarsely grated
½ small red capsicum, thinly sliced

Method

1. In a medium bowl combine 1 teaspoon of the sugar, the salt and pepper, ½ teaspoon rice vinegar, 2 teaspoons soy and the garlic. Add the steaks, mix to coat and set aside for at least 30 minutes. Stir occasionally.

2. Meanwhile, combine the honey with 2 teaspoons of sesame oil in a small bowl and set aside.

3. Heat a grilling pan or skillet to medium–high.

4. Lightly pat the steaks with paper towel to remove excess marinade. Brush each side with the honey mixture.

5. Grill the steaks for 2–3 minutes on each side, until browned and cooked to taste.

6. Make a dressing by combining the remaining sugar, rice vinegar, soy and sesame oil.

7. Mix the lettuce, zucchini (courgette) and capsicum in a bowl. Toss the dressing through. Place the salad on serving plates and top with the steaks.

Fillet of beef with creamed vegetables

25 MINUTES • SERVES 2

Ingredients

1 medium potato, diced
1 small carrot, diced
1 small zucchini (courgette), diced
100 g broccoli, diced
500 ml (2 cups) vegetable or chicken stock
2 x 175 g Scotch or eye fillet steaks, of even thickness, at least 2 cm
1 teaspoon extra-virgin olive oil
salt and freshly ground black pepper
2 tablespoons butter
1 tablespoon cream

Method

1. Place the potato, carrot, zucchini (courgette), broccoli and stock in a medium saucepan. Cover with a lid and bring to the boil. Lower the heat. Simmer for 10 minutes, until well cooked.

2. Meanwhile, coat both sides of the steaks with the oil and season with the salt and pepper.

3. Heat a medium non-stick frying pan and cook the steaks over high heat for 2–3 minutes on each side for medium–rare, until cooked to taste (*see* p. 82).

4. Drain the vegetables and return them to the saucepan. Mash roughly with a potato masher. Season with the salt and pepper, add the butter and cream, and stir to combine.

5. Place the vegetables on serving plates. Top with the steak and serve.

Sweet and spicy pork spare ribs

45 MINUTES • SERVES 2

Ingredients

4 tablespoons sweet chilli sauce
2 tablespoon soy sauce
500 g pork spare ribs, cut to fit the pan
1 small brown onion, quartered
1 beef stock cube

Method

1. In a small bowl mix the sweet chilli sauce with the soy sauce and set aside.

2. Place the ribs, onion and stock in a large saucepan of hot water. Cover with a lid and bring to the boil. Lower the heat and simmer for 30 minutes, until tender.

3. Meanwhile, preheat the grill to medium. Line the base of a grill tray with foil.

4. Remove the pork from the pan and dry with paper towel. Baste both sides with half of the sweet chilli mixture. Place under the grill and cook for 3 minutes on each side, until browned.

5. Serve with vegetables of your choice and the remaining sauce on the side.

To see this recipe visit
'Caravan Chef' on YouTube

How to cook mussels

Mussels are delicious, healthy, easy to cook and available most of the year. But the best news about mussels is their nutritional value. They are an excellent source of protein, are low in calories and fat, and contain a number of minerals and vitamins. Rich in iron, calcium, phosphorous, selenium, zinc and vitamin B12, they are also an excellent source of omega-3 fatty acids.

Mussels must be alive when bought and cooked. Fresh mussels are moist and shiny, have the tantalising smell of the sea, and their shells should be fully closed. It's best to cook mussels soon after purchase. However, under proper conditions, they should stay fresh for 2–3 days. The best way to store mussels is in a dish covered with a damp cloth or wet newspaper, and placed in the coldest part of the refrigerator. Never place them in a tightly sealed container or in water, as that will kill them. Fresh mussels are NOT suitable for freezing.

Opinions still vary as to the safety of eating unopened, cooked mussels, and some people opt to discard those. Others see them as merely more vigorous with a reluctance to open, needing extra cooking time. Once cooked open, their gender is revealed. Males turn a white–cream colour, and the females orange. A popular way of cooking mussels is to steam them with garlic, parsley and wine.

Basic steamed mussels

Ingredients

1 kg mussels
1 tablespoon extra-virgin olive oil
3 garlic cloves, finely chopped
3 tablespoons fresh parsley, coarsely chopped
190 ml (¾ cup) dry white wine

Method

1. It's best to clean the mussels just before cooking. Submerge the mussels in a bowl of cold water.

2. Clean the mussels under running cold water scrubbing vigorously with a stiff brush. That eliminates any grit, dirt or barnacles.

3. With a sharp tug, remove the long clump of brown fibres commonly known as the beard, though cultured mussels are often sold with the beards already removed.

4. Heat the oil and garlic in a large deep saucepan and sauté over low heat for 1 minute, until the garlic sizzles and becomes fragrant.

5. Stir in the parsley, wine and the mussels, and season with the salt and pepper. Cover with a lid and bring to the boil. Lower the heat to medium and cook without lifting the lid for 2–4 minutes, until the mussels open fully. Shake the pan occasionally to help open the shells.

Mussels with tomato broth and crusty bread

20 MINUTES • SERVES 2

Ingredients

1 tablespoon extra-virgin olive oil
3 garlic cloves, finely chopped
200 g can diced tomatoes
3 tablespoons fresh flat-leaf parsley, coarsely chopped
125 ml (½ cup) dry white wine
1 kg mussels, cleaned (*see* p. 95, steps 1–3)
salt and freshly ground black pepper
crusty bread, to serve

Method

1. Heat the oil and garlic in a large deep saucepan and sauté over low heat for 1 minute, until the garlic sizzles and becomes fragrant.

2. Add the tomatoes with their juice and bring to the boil. Lower the heat and simmer for 3 minutes, stirring until the sauce thickens and reduces slightly.

3. Stir in the parsley, wine and the mussels, and season with the salt and pepper. Cover with a lid and bring to the boil. Lower the heat to medium and cook without lifting the lid for 2–4 minutes, until the mussels open fully. Shake the pan occasionally to help open the shells.

4. Serve immediately with the tomato broth and crusty bread on the side.

Microwaved steamed perch with Thai-style dressing

Ingredients

3 teaspoons fish sauce
3 teaspoons lime juice, freshly squeezed
2 teaspoons brown sugar
2 medium perch fillets
5 g butter, cut into small portions
salt and freshly ground black pepper
4 slices of lemon
3 medium lettuce leaves, shredded
1 small Lebanese cucumber, thinly sliced
225 g can pineapple pieces, drained
1 tablespoon fresh coriander, coarsely chopped

Method

1. To make the dressing, combine the fish sauce, lime juice and sugar, and set aside.

2. Lightly pat the fish fillets dry with paper towel to remove excess moisture. Dot each fillet with butter and season with the salt and pepper. Place two slices of lemon on top of each fillet.

3. Place the fish in a microwave steamer. Cover with a lid. Cook in the microwave on medium power for 3 minutes. Uncover, being mindful of hot steam, and check how much of the flesh has turned white. Cook for up to 2 minutes longer, until the fish is flaked and cooked through.

4. Meanwhile, place the lettuce, cucumber, pineapple and coriander in a mixing bowl and combine, then season with the salt and pepper.

5. Place the fish on serving plates. Arrange with the salad on the side and drizzle with the dressing.

Pan-fried salmon with avocado and asparagus

20 MINUTES • SERVES 2

Ingredients

2 fresh salmon steaks
1½ teaspoons extra-virgin olive oil
salt and freshly ground black pepper
1 bunch asparagus, trimmed and cut into 5 cm lengths
1 avocado, sliced
1 tablespoon capers, drained
1 garlic clove, chopped
1 tablespoon fresh parsley, chopped
½ lime, zested and juiced

Method

1. Lightly pat the salmon dry with paper towel to remove excess moisture. Coat both sides with ½ teaspoon of the oil and, just prior to cooking, season with the salt and pepper.

2. Heat a medium deep non-stick frying pan over medium heat.

3. Place the salmon in the pan, skin-side down. Cook for 3 minutes, until the base of the salmon becomes golden and crispy, and the flesh turns opaque a third of the way up from the base of the fillet.

4. Turn with a spatula and cook the other side for 2 minutes, until the base browns and the flesh changes colour, except for a thin line in the middle.

5. Meanwhile, cook the asparagus in boiling water for 2 minutes, until just tender. Drain.

6. Place the asparagus, avocado, capers, garlic, parsley, lime juice and the remaining oil in a bowl, and stir to combine.

7. Make a bed of vegetables on serving plates. Place the salmon on top, sprinkle with the lime zest and serve.

Seafood bake

Ingredients

1 medium green zucchini (courgette), sliced diagonally
1 bunch baby broccoli, trimmed and cut into three lengths
200 g yellow squash, cut into wedges
100 g grape tomatoes
2 garlic cloves, chopped
1 tablespoon extra-virgin olive oil
200 g fresh red salmon, cut into large bite-sized pieces
4 large green banana prawns, unpeeled
6 scallops
1 lemon, cut into wedges
salt and freshly ground black pepper

Method

1. Preheat a fan-forced oven to 200°C (conventional oven 220°C/Gas 6).

2. In a medium bowl combine the zucchini (courgette), broccoli, squash, tomatoes, garlic and 2 teaspoons of the oil. Stir to coat and place evenly in a baking tray.

3. Scatter the salmon, prawns and scallops evenly over the top of the vegetables. Drizzle with the remaining oil and the juice from two lemon wedges. Add the juiced lemon wedges to the tray for extra flavour and season with the salt and pepper.

4. Lower the oven to 180°C (conventional oven 200°C/Gas 4). Bake for 20 minutes, until the seafood is cooked through and the vegetables are tender. Stir once during the cooking process.

5. Serve with the remaining lemon wedges on the side.

Grilled swordfish with avocado salsa

15 MINUTES • SERVES 2

Ingredients

2 swordfish fillets
½ teaspoon extra-virgin olive oil
salt and freshly ground black pepper
1 large avocado, diced
1 small ripe tomato, seeded and chopped
½ small red onion, diced
1 tablespoon lime or lemon juice, freshly squeezed
1 tablespoon sweet chilli sauce
1 tablespoon coriander, chopped (optional)

Method

1. Lightly pat the swordfish dry with paper towel to remove excess moisture. Coat both sides with oil and season with the salt and pepper.

2. Preheat the grill to medium–high. Place the fish on the grill and cook for 2–3 minutes, until the base of the swordfish browns and the flesh changes colour a third of the way up from the base.

3. Turn with a spatula and cook the other side for 2–3 minutes, until the remaining flesh colours, except for a thin line in the middle.

4. To make the salsa, in a medium bowl combine the avocado, tomato, onion, lime or lemon juice, sweet chilli sauce and coriander, if using, and season with the salt and pepper.

5. Arrange the salsa on serving plates. Place the fish on top and serve.

Sweet treats

Berrymisu

Ingredients

410 g can strawberries, drained, reserving the juice
300 ml thickened cream
1 tablespoon caster sugar
150 g packet sponge finger biscuits

Method

1. Line a loaf-sized dish to the rim with foil.

2. In a small bowl combine the strawberries with 2 tablespoons of the juice. Puree or mash with a fork.

3. Place the cream and sugar in the bowl of an electric mixer and whisk for 1 minute, until thickened.

4. Arrange a single layer of biscuits over the base of the dish. Drizzle 6 tablespoons of the reserved juice over the biscuits. Spread half of the cream evenly over the biscuits. Spoon half of the pureed strawberries over the top.

5. Repeat with a second layer. Discard any remaining juice.

6. Refrigerate overnight.

7. Lift out with the foil, cut into slices and serve cold.

Pavlova with berries

45 MINUTES • SERVES 4

Ingredients

4 egg whites
200 g (1 cup) caster sugar
½ teaspoon vanilla essence
1 teaspoon white vinegar
300 ml thickened cream
1 punnet strawberries, trimmed and halved
1 punnet blueberries

Method

1. Preheat a fan-forced oven to 170˚C (conventional oven 190˚C/Gas 3).

2. Line the bottom of a baking tray with baking paper.

3. Place the egg whites in the bowl of an electric mixer. Beat on high speed for 2–3 minutes, adding a little of the sugar at a time, until the mixture forms stiff peaks.

4. With a spatula gently fold in the vanilla and the vinegar. Pile the mixture into four separate domes on the baking tray.

5. Lower the oven to 150˚C (conventional oven 170˚C/Gas 2). Bake for 15 minutes.

6. Lower the oven to 130˚C (conventional oven 150˚C/Gas 2). Bake for a further 15 minutes, until lightly browned on top and cooked through.

7. Remove from the oven and let stand in the tray for 10 minutes, until cool.

8. Place the cream in the bowl of an electric mixer and whisk for 1 minute, until thickened.

9. Top each pavlova dome with cream. Arrange the fruit over the top and serve.

Apricot custard

35 MINUTES • SERVES 2

Ingredients

410 g can apricot halves, drained, reserving the juice to serve
1 egg, lightly beaten
1½ tablespoons caster sugar
150 ml cream
¼ teaspoon vanilla essence
1 teaspoon ground nutmeg, to serve (optional)
maple syrup, to serve (optional)

Method

1 Preheat a fan-forced oven to 170˚C (conventional oven 190˚C/Gas 3).

2 Arrange apricots, without overlapping, in a 15 cm x 20 cm ovenproof dish.

3 In a small bowl combine the egg, sugar, cream and vanilla. Pour over the apricots. Sprinkle with nutmeg, if using, and bake for 25–30 minutes, until the custard has set. Cool slightly for easier cutting.

4 Place the custard on serving plates. Serve topped with the maple syrup, if using, and reserved juice from the apricots.

Fruit tempura

Ingredients

1 egg, lightly whisked
200 ml iced water
90 g (¾ cup) plain (all-purpose) flour, sifted
¼ teaspoon salt
vegetable oil, for frying
1 medium apple, peeled, cored and cut into 16 wedges
2 small bananas, peeled, halved lengthwise and cut into 3
2 tablespoons icing sugar, sifted

Method

1. Combine the egg and water in a small, deep mixing bowl. Gradually stir in the flour and salt, until combined to a thin, lightly creamy consistency. It is acceptable for the batter to be slightly lumpy.

2. Pour oil into a large saucepan to a depth of 3 cm and heat until a drop of batter added to it sizzles.

3. Using tongs, dip each piece of fruit in the batter until coated and then gently submerge in the hot oil. Repeat until the saucepan is filled with a single layer of fruit, spaced well apart. Cook for 1–2 minutes, until the batter sets, turning once. Remove the fruit and drain on paper towel.

4. Use a slotted spoon to skim off any batter from the hot oil before repeating the process with the remaining fruit. Ensure that the oil remains hot.

5. Dust the fruit with the icing sugar and serve.

Cook's notes

Cook's notes

MEASUREMENTS Ingredients are measured to Australian Standard Metric system. All cup and spoon measurements are level.

ESTIMATED COOKING TIME The estimated time needed to cook a recipe begins when all the ingredients are assembled in the suggested quantities, ready for peeling (if specified) chopping or cooking. Whenever possible, water for boiling vegetables or cooking dry pasta or rice, was boiled in an electric jug prior to cooking, to save time.

Cooking times may vary depending on width of pans, the type and size of hotplates, the type of heat, electric or gas, and pressure of the gas, if using.

Ingredients

VEGETABLES Washing fruit and vegetables is the cook's responsibility, and not part of my written instructions. All potatoes, carrots, zucchini and pumpkin should be peeled before cutting or grating, unless specified otherwise such as in 'Roast vegetable penne'.

BUTTER Salted or unsalted if preferred.

CREAM Fresh pouring cream is used throughout the recipes unless specified as thickened cream.

PEPPER I favour freshly ground black pepper. Shop ground can be used.

Cookware and utensils

PANS Generally, for ease of cooking and cleaning, I favour using non-stick frying pans and saucepans. When cooking curries, casseroles or onions where caramelising is required, I use saucepans with a heavy base, such as cast-iron ones. Clear lids are particularly helpful in monitoring the cooking process. Most recipes require a medium saucepan, 18–20 cm in diameter, and a medium frying pan, 24 cm in diameter.

KNIVES I use a range of knives. By far the most important one is my all-purpose 15 cm cook's knife. The price of a good quality knife is money well spent. Ensure that the knife sits well in your hand and feels balanced. A small vegetable knife is also a must. Keep your knives in good order by hand-washing them after use and keeping them sharp.

CHOPPING BOARDS For hygienic purposes, I favour colour-coded chopping boards: green for vegetables, red for meat, blue for seafood and white for general and cheese. Using single-purpose boards prevents food contamination by transferring juices from raw meat onto other food preparation surfaces.

I use wooden and thin plastic boards, for ease and practicality. They are light-weight, and store and wash easily. Whether wooden or plastic, make sure they are regularly washed or replaced. Glass, ceramic and stone chopping boards are not knife-friendly as they tend to blunt the blade.

MIXING BOWLS A set of small, medium and large mixing bowls is a must (small 10–16 cm, medium 18–20 cm and large 24–26 cm). Most of my recipes require a medium bowl.

A TIMER I find timers very useful and own three for convenience. That allows me the freedom to walk away from the cooking area without compromising the recipe.

ELECTRIC MIXERS I find a handheld electric mixer sufficient to make all the sweet recipes in my cookbooks.

THERMAL COOKING POTS Thermal cooking pots are useful for preparing meals in advance. After cooking on the stove for 5–20 minutes, the inner cooking pot is locked in the insulated host pot and left to rest for 1–4 hours. During that time the trapped heat continues to cook the food, and the pot should not be opened. The thermal cooking pot used in this book has an inside diameter of 20 cm.

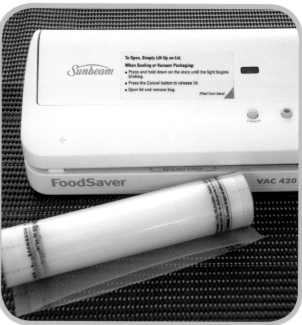

Storage

FRIDGE THERMOMETER Because the fridge is such an integral part of healthy food preparation, it should be monitored carefully. With frequent opening of the fridge door and changes in room temperature it's often difficult to know if the fridge is maintaining its correct temperature. I suggest you place a fridge thermometer in your fridge. It's the best way to know that you're storing your refrigerated food at a healthy temperature. The readout should show clearly whether the fridge is operating within the safe range. The Food Safety Information Council recommends the temperature be at 5 degrees Celsius or just below.

VACUUM SEALING Prolongs freshness and fridge life, it also allows for purchasing a range of meats and cheese in advance, or in bulk to save money, and portion for later use. I travel with a compact machine that's perfectly suited to caravanning and I keep a larger model at home.

PLASTIC CONTAINERS Plastic containers are handy as they are light, easy to store, and serve many purposes. Apart from pantry and fridge storage, some can be used for preparation in cooking such as marinating or cooking in a microwave, but ensure that they are heat resistant.

FLOUR, PASTA AND RICE To ensure freshness and dryness of dry goods such as flour, pasta and rice, store them in airtight plastic containers. Label similar-looking ingredients such as plain (all-purpose) or self-rising flour, to eliminate confusion.

VEGETABLES If your fridge does not have a crisper drawer, airtight plastic containers are useful to store fresh vegetables. Cut vegetables to fit the container, cover tightly with the lid and refrigerate. That includes heads of lettuce which can be peeled and stored as leaves.

LETTUCE If your fridge is not big enough to take a plastic bubble container for heads of lettuce, don't despair. Peel the lettuce off, rinse under cold water, shake off excess moisture, and stack in a plastic container with an airtight lid. They should last in the fridge for up to a week.

MEAT, FISH AND CHEESE When purchasing meat, fish, sliced ham or cheese, I portion them into recipe-size or manageable quantities and vacuum seal them. I then label the packets with the date and contents, to eliminate confusion.

POTATOES, ONIONS, GARLIC AND WHOLE PUMPKIN Store in a cool, dark, dry and well-ventilated place.

EGGS It has been recommended that eggs are refrigerated for maximum freshness or store them in a cool, dry place. In a refrigerated environment they may last up to five weeks, but that time frame lessens drastically as temperatures increase. It is important to test any unrefrigerated eggs before consuming. Submerge the egg in a cup of water at room temperature. A fresh egg will sink to the bottom. If the egg floats, it is no longer fresh and should not be eaten.

The 30 ingredients
from my previous 'Caravan Chef' cookbooks

SALT Sea salt is my favourite. If preferred, a salt substitute may be used.

OLIVE OIL I use cold-pressed extra-virgin olive oil.

PLAIN (ALL-PURPOSE) FLOUR

CORNFLOUR A great thickening agent.

CHICKEN STOCK Can be homemade, bought diluted, powdered or in cubes.

CURRY POWDER

SOY SAUCE Can be Chinese, Japanese, light or dark (for a fuller flavour and colour), low salt if preferred.

SWEET CHILLI SAUCE

SALAD DRESSING Extra-virgin olive oil vinaigrette and balsamic dressing are my favourite.

MAYONNAISE Low or full fat.

PASTA Long and short pasta, fresh or dried, and instant noodles.

RICE Arborio or basmati.

EGGS Only free range for me.

CHEESE Hard cheddar or parmesan are versatile and grate well.

CHICKEN FILLETS Fillets of loin, thigh or breast.

MEAT I choose lean or 'heart smart' cuts of beef, lamb, veal or pork.

HAM I buy loosely sliced ham, portion it, and seal it in a vacuum-sealing machine for prolonged freshness.

FISH Fresh fish fillets are my favourite.

CANNED TOMATOES I recommend Italian diced tomatoes.

FRESH TOMATOES I buy truss or vine-ripened for flavour.

PEAS Fresh or frozen.

GARLIC Fresh is best.

ONIONS Brown onions store well, white are milder than brown. In salads I like red onions for colour.

POTATOES Pontiacs are good all-rounders.

LETTUCE

CARROTS

CAPSICUM Red are sweeter than green.

ZUCCHINI (COURGETTE)

PUMPKIN I buy butternut for easy cutting.

CAULIFLOWER

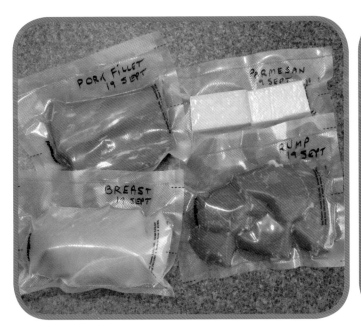

Conversions

LIQUID MEASUREMENTS
5 ml = 1 teaspoon
20 ml = 1 tablespoon
250 ml = 1 cup

BUTTER
5 g = 1 teaspoon
16 g = 1 tablespoon
65 g = 4 tablespoons

CHEESE
10 g = 1 tablespoon grated cheddar
   or parmesan
80 g = 1 cup grated cheddar or parmesan

FLOUR
10 g = 1 tablespoon
120 g = 1 cup

FRUIT
1 small apple = 125 g
1 medium apple = 225 g
1 small banana = 100 g
1 punnet blueberries = 125 g
1 punnet strawberries = 250 g

OLIVES
80 g olives = ½ cup

PICKLED DILL CUCUMBERS
1 small = 50 g

PINE NUTS
14 g = 1 tablespoon

PUMPKIN
375 g fresh pumpkin in 2 cm
   cubes = 1 cup roast pumpkin

750 g fresh pumpkin in 2 cm cubes =
   2 cups roast pumpkin

RICE
200 g long-grain = 1 cup
220 g aborio = 1 cup
1 cup rice = 3 cups cooked rice

SHORT PASTA
100 g = 1 cup
85 g risoni = ½ cup

SMALL NOODLES
50 g = ½ cup

SUGAR
16 g caster = 1 tablespoon
200 g caster = 1 cup

2 g raw = ½ teaspoon
5 g raw = 1 teaspoon
18 g raw = 1 tablespoon
73 g raw = 4 tablespoons
73 g raw = ⅓ cup

VEGETABLES

1 bunch asparagus = 150 g
1 bunch baby broccoli = 215 g
1 small broccoli = 150 g
¼ cabbage = 450 g
1 small capsicum = 120 g
1 medium capsicum = 200 g
1 small carrot = 100 g
1 medium carrot = 150 g

1 medium cucumber = 150 g
1 cup shredded lettuce = 60 g
1 small lettuce leaf = 40 g
1 medium lettuce leaf = 60 g
1 small onion = 80 g
1 medium onion = 140 g
1 tablespoon fresh peas = 10 g
1 small potato = 100 g
1 medium potato = 150 g
1 small sweet potato = 100 g
1 cup baby rocket = 45 g
1 small tomato = 100 g
1 medium tomato = 150 g
1 small zucchini (courgette) = 100 g
1 medium zucchini (courgette) = 150 g

Index

About the author

Most people know Eva as the 'Caravan Chef', a happy fellow traveller who also loves to cook; however, she's also a wife, mother and grandmother, living in the suburbs of bustling Sydney.

Accompanied by her husband Thom, Eva Stovern has travelled all over Australia by caravan. She enjoys scouring grocery shops in small country towns and sitting down to a home-cooked meal in front of a fiery outback sunset, far removed from restaurants and city life. Enterprising and passionate, Eva's travel and passion for cooking has resulted in three successful cookbooks called 'The Caravan Chef'. Eva has also contributed editorial content for many popular travel publications and websites, as well as appearing in cooking segments on TV shows. In addition to this, Eva has her own website (www.caravanchef.com) where she shares travel and cooking tips.

Acknowledgements

To my publishers Astrid and Melissa, a big thank you for your faith and continuing support. I'm grateful for Emma and Alison's skilful editing, and for Julie's artistic design. To Natasha, thanks for capturing my meals so beautifully with your creative eye.

Loving thanks to my husband Thom, who continues to praise and support me in my ventures, you are my essential ingredient. Many thanks to dear Kylie, the chef who was there in the beginning with her invaluable advice. To my artist friend John Wyndus, for his inspiration to write my first book, and also for designing my lovable logo.

And to my lovely daughters, Tania and Natalie, whose smiling faces always give me strength.

Acknowledgements

The publisher would like to acknowledge the following individuals and organisations:

Editorial manager
Melissa Kayser

Project manager
Alison Proietto

Editor
Emma Adams

Design and layout
Penny Black Design

Photography
Natasha Milne

Index
Max McMaster

Pre-press
Splitting Image

With thanks to Jayco Sydney for supplying the Jayco Silverline caravan as featured on the front and back covers.

Explore Australia Publishing Pty Ltd
Ground Floor, Building 1, 658 Church Street, Richmond, VIC 3121

Explore Australia Publishing Pty Ltd is a division of Hardie Grant Publishing Pty Ltd

hardie grant publishing

Published by Explore Australia Publishing Pty Ltd, 2015

ISBN-13 9781741174670

10 9 8 7 6 5 4 3 2 1

A Cataloguing-in-Publication entry is available from the catalogue of the National Library of Australia at www.nla.gov.au

Printed and bound in China by 1010 Printing International Ltd

Disclaimer: This book uses metric cup measurements, i.e. 250 ml for 1 cup; in the US 1 cup is 8 fl oz, just smaller, and American cooks should be generous in their cup measurements; in the UK 1 cup is 10 fl oz, and British cooks should be scant with their cup measurements.

www.exploreaustralia.net.au
Follow us on Twitter: @ExploreAus
Find us on Facebook: www.facebook.com/
 exploreaustralia